TAKE TEN

TAKE TEN

THE ADULT TIMEOUT

Cynthia Chauvin
with Miles Chauvin

TAKE TEN

The Adult Timeout

ISBN 13: 978-1-62154-495-1

Cover and Interior Design by Nu-ImageDesign.com

Image Copyright Billdayone, 2012

Used under license from Shutterstock.com

Author photography: Joe Henson

Bebas font courtesy: Ryoichi Tsunekawa

Published by:

Two Dragons International Inc.

Washington D.C. | New Orleans

www.twodragons.com

For special pricing on bulk sales contact

booksales@twodragons.com

For more information and companion audio products please visit

Cynthia's website:

www.cynthiachauvin.com

FOREWORD

My wife Cynthia has done thousands of psychic readings and hypnosis sessions for her clients. The insights in *Take Ten* come from these experiences.

This book and the other books in the *Take Ten* series along with *The 10 Ways*, and our audio CDs are all designed to empower you with the tools to change unproductive thoughts and behaviors.

Whether you use the products together, or separately, the information in each will help you have a better relationship with yourself and others.

Miles Chauvin

INTRODUCTION

Every behavior pattern you have created, started out with a base positive intent to protect you. The behavior may now be antiquated and no longer work to help you, but the intent still holds true.

The power to change these old behaviors lies in your ability to interrupt the patterns in your life and replace them with a broader perspective.

Take Ten was created to be a pattern interrupter, a simple yet effective way to take the moment before an unwanted behavior is repeated and instead fill that moment with insight.

These insights allow you to rethink your present course of action thereby opening you to more choices.

When you see new choices on how to experience a situation, you change your experience. Once an experience is changed, behavior is changed and thereby the outcome changes.

Changes are ecological. When you change one tiny part everything else starts to align itself with that new part. There is no such thing as a small change – it all has a big impact.

HOW TO USE THIS BOOK

The idea is of this book is to literally take ten.

When you feel yourself drifting into a sea of depleting, derogatory or unsuccessful repetitive behavior take the book out and think to your self:

"What am I trying to see at this moment? How does this experience want to help me?"

Then flip to a page.

Drink the insight in and let it propagate and inform your thoughts about the situation you are dealing with.

"

We have a memory so we don't stick our hand in the fire again, not to judge ourselves for sticking it in the first time.

"

"

Victim. Martyr. Perpetrator. When these three children grow up they become Compassion, Wisdom and Strength.

"

Faith allows you to feel love.

"

We whisper our knowledge, and shout our ignorance.

"

"

Dig soft, but dig.

"

There is only one virus: shame.

"

Consciousness flows like a river. Sometimes we dam this river with denial.

"

"

People are our enablers, not our creators. They enable us to see what we create.

"

It is easy to think we have succeeded when things are good and the environment supports us. But life consists of many twists and turns, and success comes from seeing the success in all of it.

"

When you speak lies, others can lie to you. When you speak the truth, no one can lie to you.

"

"

All we need to do to live life fully is show up, shut up, and open up.

"

"

When a heart breaks, it opens to new possibilities, as long as we don't fall prey to ego's encouragement that all is not heaven-sent.

"

"

I llusion is in the eye of the beholder.

"

"

K indness grows on the tree of acceptance.

"

"

I am a spirit that has feelings, emotions, a mind and body. I am not feelings, emotions, mind and body that have a spirit.

"

"

The sooner we figure out we own nothing, the sooner we will stop fighting over it.

"

People are complicated; wisdom is simple.

"

What I do is about who I wish to be; how it is used in the world is not up to me.

"

"

Who died and left you my creator? Oh, it must have been me.

"

"

We contain information, not possess it.

"

"

The road to enlightenment is the one you are on.

"

"

Warm yourself with memories,
but fuel yourself with God.

"

"

Know who you are, know your reality.

"

"

There is no greater power than
to know All is One.

"

"

What is a pedestal? A place from which to fall.

"

"

Place no God before you. Put your ego second, and God first.

"

R epetition is a gift to awaken the sleeper within.

"

You can't own what belongs to everyone.

"

"

Everybody is our equal; however everyone is not our peer.

"

"

Once some aspect of ourselves is noticed, it can no longer sleep.

"

"

We utilize our environment to excuse our behavior.

"

"

Scientists have proven the world is flat.

"

"

R eality is actually real for the moment.

"

"

Detachment isn't lack of action or concern, but the trust to stop trying to control the outcome.

"

"

Forever ye shall walk in the Valley of Death until ye fear no evil.

"

"

We are all the light, just different wattages.

"

"

To be or not to be is still the question.

"

"

The list of things to fear is as long as the one to love.

"

"

Everyone has a destiny - the grandest expression of his or her soul. And everyone reaches it. Absolutely everyone.

"

"

Without Faith we are all fools.

"

"

Parents are for the most part just older children.

"

"

Fear is a decision. So is Love.

"

"

Science is opinion waiting to be disproved.

"

"

Sometimes we have to walk through the briar patch to get to the meadow.

"

"

The reason why someone says, "I would do anything for you" is because they want to be able to expect anything from you.

"

"

We all need to detach from the image of ourselves to find the meaning of ourselves.

"

If you believe it, don't teach it. Just be it.

"

P roof is never in the end result it is in the faith.

"

"

Where faith shines, darkness turns to wisdom.

"

"

When "me" opens it turns to "we."

"

"

Today's judgments ten years down the road turn into assessments. Assessments ten years down the road will be seen as judgments.

"

"

We limit ourselves to the point we can digest the current feelings, thoughts, information. Then we produce a larger vision.

"

"

Where there is no communication we go to war.

"

"

Your past is not for nothing. Your future is not for sure. Your present is a combination of both. Add a little faith to it, and you will find today.

"

"

We forget Who We Are to remember Who We Are.

"

"

My inner vision is clear: I know that I don't know.

"

"

To use your mind and not your spirit is like driving a car from the back seat. You get nowhere fast.

"

"

To build integrity of the mind, ask how, what, where, when, why. To build integrity of the spirit, realize the need of the mind to know how, what, where, when and why is unnecessary.

"

"

E go is the creation of God's experience in duality, -beautiful, but just a small piece.

"

"

No one single event makes a person, no one single event destroys a person.

"

"

The whole human race is joint tenants in common.

"

"

The moon lights the night, sun lights the day, and Love lights the heart.

"

"

Guilt numbs us to our fears.

"

"

If we stay busy discovering ourselves, we have no time to try and fix what isn't broken.

"

"

Everyone says just be who you are. We better find out who that is first.

"

"

As far as I can see is as far as I can see.

"

"

Create wisdom, and peace will reign.

"

"

We must decide we do not have to make up our mind. We have to find our mind.

"

"

What we learn today comes from remembering something we already knew.

"

"

Cause is internal. Effect is external.

"

"

P arents make us unimportant, children make us all-important, and God makes us equally important.

"

"

All manipulation is self-manipulation.

"

"

Everything has a purpose, every purpose has a reason, and every reason has a gift - the gift being we don't need to know the purpose.

"

"

Fear or Love. Pick one.

"

"

M emory was made so we can relate our experiences of the Eternal Now to each other.

"

"

Dare you to be honest. Double dare ya.

"

"

Emotions are like icebergs. What you can see is just the tip of what's really there.

"

"

Duality is not reality.

"

"

Conclusions are illusions.

"

"

If you fight over what's right, you don't know what's right.

"

"

Life is loving your own warts, laughing at your own corny jokes and finding love in all of it.

"

"

L et's love each other for our difference; it gives us a bigger picture of ourselves.

"

"

Wishes come true. Do you know what you wish for - or do you find out after you received it?

"

"

The past should be used like a rear view mirror.

"

"

He who accuses is the one who abuses.

"

"

Fatigue and anger make a cocktail called "Bad Decision."

"

"

We rewrite our history and rewrite our history until we realize we write our history.

"

"

To forgive takes one; to reconcile takes two.

"

"

You can't out run yourself.

"

"

The familiar bad of today is better than the unknown happiness of tomorrow.

"

"

Science exists because man wants to play God before becoming God.

"

"

Judgments of others limit self-knowledge.

"

"

A teacher doesn't teach, they reflect.

"

"

If you do not think you made a wrong choice you can make another choice. But if you think you made a wrong choice you will make the same choice.

"

"

Neediness is an expression of childishness. Passion is an expression of love.

"

K eep focus on the joy in your day and the joy in your life will unfold.

"

We live in a state of lack in a world of abundance.

"

"

I am of one mind and that is I am the Divine.

"

"

You never get rid of old thoughts you only expand them.

"

"

You can recognize progress and then not be stung by repetitiveness.

"

"

To live from love grows the only life untarnished.

"

"

Today's lies are yesterday's truths.

"

"

I have no illusions that I live in an illusion.

"

"

It is only our disbelief in ourselves, a lack of knowing who we are, that causes difficulties in our lives.

"

"

One person's full plate is another person's half.

"

"

Usually the anxiety in a relationship is not about your present relationship, it is about your past experience.

"